Aug 2019

D1126536

SOCCER STARS

CRISTIANO
RONALDO

BRIANNA BATTISTA

PowerKiDS press™

New York

Published in 2019 by The Rosen Publishing Group, Inc.
29 East 21st Street, New York, NY 10010

First Edition

Editor: Elizabeth Krajnik
Book Design: Michael Flynn

Photo Credits: Cover (Ronaldo), p. 1 NurPhoto/Getty Images; cover (stadium background) winui/Shutterstock.com; cover (player glow) Nejron Photo/Shutterstock.com; pp. 3, 23, 24 (background) Narong Jongsirikul/Shutterstock.com; pp. 4, 6, 8–10, 12, 14, 16–18, 20, 22 (ball background) DRN Studio/Shutterstock.com; p. 5 Chris Brunskill Ltd/Getty Images Sport/Getty Images; p. 7 Karwai Tang/Wirelmage/Getty Images; p. 8 GREGORIO CUNHA/AFP/Getty Images; p. 9 Julio Azevedo/Icon Sport/Getty Images; p. 11 LLUIS GENE/AFP/Getty Images; p. 13 ADRIAN DENNIS/AFP/Getty Images; p. 14 Christopher Lee/Getty Images Sport/Getty Images; p. 15 Kiyoshi Ota/Getty Images Sport/Getty Images; p. 16 Ross Kinnaird/Getty Images Sport/Getty Images; p. 17 Matthew Peters/Manchester United/Getty Images; p. 18 Maxisport/Shutterstock.com; p. 19 Matt Trommer/Shutterstock.com; p. 21 Mustafa Yalcin/Anadolu Agency/Getty Images; p. 22 Laszlo Szirtesi/Shutterstock.com.

Cataloging-in-Publication Data

Names: Battista, Brianna.
Title: Cristiano Ronaldo / Brianna Battista.
Description: New York : PowerKids Press, 2019. | Series: Soccer stars | Includes glossary and index.
Identifiers: ISBN 9781538344729 (pbk.) | ISBN 9781538343487 (library bound) | ISBN 9781538344736 (6 pack)
Subjects: LCSH: Ronaldo, Cristiano, 1985–Juvenile literature. | Soccer players–Portugal–Biography–Juvenile literature.
Classification: LCC GV942.7.R626 B325 2019 | DDC 796.334092 B–dc23

Manufactured in the United States of America

CPSIA Compliance Information: Batch #CWPK19 For Further Information contact Rosen Publishing, New York, New York at 1-800-237-9932

CONTENTS

INTRODUCING RONALDO!

Do you like soccer? Perhaps you play on a school team or maybe you watch it at home with your family. Soccer is a popular sport all over the world. Cristiano Ronaldo is a Portuguese **professional** soccer player. He plays the position of forward for Real Madrid, a Spanish club team, and the Portuguese national team.

Ronaldo stands out for how many goals he has scored, his control of the soccer ball, and being a powerful leader. Many people think of Ronaldo as the best player of his **generation**. Other people think he's the greatest player of all time. In this book, we'll take a close look at Ronaldo's **career**.

STAR POWER

Ronaldo's full name is Cristiano Ronaldo dos Santos Aviero. "Ronaldo" was given to him as a middle name in honor of Ronald Reagan, Ronaldo's father's favorite actor.

ON APRIL 11, 2018, REAL MADRID PLAYED AGAINST JUVENTUS IN A SECOND-LEG MATCH OF THE UEFA CHAMPIONS LEAGUE QUARTER FINAL AT ESTADIO SANTIAGO BERNABÉU IN MADRID, SPAIN.

HUMBLE BEGINNINGS

Ronaldo was born on February 5, 1985, in the Santo Antonio neighborhood of Funchal on the Portuguese island of Madeira. The youngest of four children, Ronaldo shared a room with his brother and two sisters in their family's small house in one of the city's poorest neighborhoods.

Before Ronaldo became a soccer star, his mother, Maria Dolores dos Santos Aveiro, was a chef. His father, José Dinis Aviero, was a gardener and an equipment manager for the local soccer club Andorinha.

Because his father worked for Andorinha, the young Ronaldo spent time at the club. He would try dribbling, or running with, the ball and copying the older players.

MARIA DOLORES DOS SANTOS AVEIRO

CRISTIANO RONALDO JR.

RONALDO CAME FROM **HUMBLE** BEGINNINGS. AS A BOY, RONALDO AND HIS BROTHER AND SISTERS DIDN'T HAVE TOYS AND DIDN'T GET CHRISTMAS PRESENTS. HE IS VERY CLOSE WITH HIS MOTHER, WHO RAISED HIM TO BE VERY RELIGIOUS.

THE LITTLE BEE

Ronaldo played a lot of street soccer as a young boy and began playing for Andorinha, his first club, when he was around eight years old. Even then, Ronaldo stood out as a talented player. He was called *abelhinha*, which means "little bee" in Portuguese, because he was small and very quick on the field. Soon, other clubs noticed the little bee.

CRISTIANO RONALDO'S SOCCER ID CARD (1994–1995)

ESCOLAS

REGIONAL

ÉPOCA

94–95

ASSOCIAÇÃO DE FUTEBOL DO FUNCHAL

NOME  CRISTIANO RONALDO DOS SANTOS AVEIRO

CLUBE Clube Futebol Andorinha

LICENÇA N.º

 17.182

O SECRETÁRIO GERAL

WHEN RONALDO FIRST MOVED TO LISBON, SOME OF HIS NEW CLASSMATES MADE FUN OF HIM FOR HIS MADEIRAN ACCENT. HE HAD TO STAY STRONG FOR HIS LOVE OF THE GAME.

Within two years, Ronaldo began playing for Madeira's biggest team, Clube Desportivo Nacional of Madeira. When he was 12 years old, Ronaldo had a three-day trial with Sporting Clube de Portugal (CP) in the capital city of Lisbon. The team signed him for about $2,148.

LIFE IN LISBON

Lisbon had new **challenges** in store for Ronaldo. He moved there all by himself and felt very lonely and homesick. Ronaldo returned to Madeira and almost stayed, which would have been the end of his soccer career! However, he went back to Lisbon to keep playing for Sporting CP and promised to work and train harder than ever.

Another challenge came when Ronaldo turned 15 years old. Doctors told him he had a problem with his heart. His heartbeat raced even when he was wasn't running. Heart disease can force even the best players to quit the sport. Ronaldo's drive was so strong that he went back to his training just days after an operation to fix the problem.

STAR POWER

Ronaldo's hard work paid off. In just one season, he moved up from Sporting CP's under-16 team all the way to the first team. He was the first player to do this.

RONALDO WOULD OFTEN STAY AN EXTRA HALF HOUR AFTER TRAINING TO WORK ON THE SKILLS HE HAD A HARD TIME WITH.

BREAKTHROUGH

In 2003, Ronaldo signed with Manchester United. He was the team's first-ever Portuguese player. The team's manager, Alex Ferguson, offered Ronaldo the number 7 jersey. The most famous Manchester United players, such as David Beckham, had worn that number. Ferguson was sure Ronaldo could one day be just as good as these other players were. Ronaldo believes this was a turning point in his career. He said, "I was forced to live up to such an honor."

Ronaldo's debut, or first time playing for the team, was on August 16, 2003. He only played for 30 minutes, but he still caught the fans' attention! Fans rose to their feet clapping when he came out. Ronaldo's high energy and skill helped Manchester score another three points.

STAR POWER

To sign Ronaldo, Manchester United paid Sporting CP a transfer **fee** of more than $17.5 million! At the time, Ronaldo was the most costly teenager in British football history.

FORMER MANCHESTER UNITED PLAYER GEORGE BEST CALLED RONALDO'S FIRST GAME "THE MOST EXCITING DEBUT" HE HAD EVER SEEN.

ATTITUDE TRAINING

Ronaldo still had a lot of growing up to do before he could become the soccer star he is today. Ronaldo wanted to be the best player in the world so badly that he often got angry. He was kicked out of many important games and was kept from playing in others as a result.

Ronaldo needed to change his attitude. His coach, René Meulensteen, told him he was only playing for himself. He taught Ronaldo the importance of being a team player. He told Ronaldo, "The most important individuals are the ones who **elevate** the team, not themselves."

RENÉ MEULENSTEEN

UNDER MEULENSTEEN'S DIRECTION, RONALDO PRACTICED DRILLS TO HELP HIM SCORE MORE GOALS AND HAVE A BETTER ATTITUDE.

CR7 ON FIRE!

Ronaldo's 2007–2008 season with Manchester United ended up being one of his best. The 22-year-old scored a total of 42 goals as a right wing, which means he played **offense** on the right side of the field.

RONALDO'S NICKNAME, CR7, COMES FROM HIS INITIALS AND HIS JERSEY NUMBER.

Ronaldo started to become known for his powerful header, in which he uses his head to direct the ball into the net. He also was known for his direct free kick, which is a kick used to restart a game after a **foul**. In 2008, the Fédération Internationale de Football Association (FIFA) crowned Ronaldo World Player of the Year. Fans all over the world were cheering Ronaldo's nickname—CR7!

STAR POWER

During Ronaldo's six years playing for Manchester United, he scored a total of 118 goals and helped the team win three Premiere League championships.

REAL MADRID

In 2009, Real Madrid signed Ronaldo for a record-setting transfer fee of €94 million, which is about $131.5 million. Ronaldo now played in La Liga, the top men's professional association football division of the Spanish football league system. This meant Ronaldo would now **compete** against his top soccer **rival**, Lionel Messi. Messi plays for Barcelona and is one of the league's leading goal scorers.

During the 2010–2011 season, Ronaldo scored 40 goals. At the time, Ronaldo was the top goal scorer in the history of the league! The following year, he helped Real Madrid win their first league championship in four years.

LIONEL MESSI

IT HAD BEEN RONALDO'S MOTHER'S DREAM TO HAVE HER SON PLAY FOR REAL MADRID.

NO STOPPING RONALDO

In 2009, Ronaldo was the runner-up to Messi for World Player of the Year. In 2010, the award was renamed the Ballon d'Or, which means "golden ball" in French. He was runner-up to Messi again in 2011, 2012, and 2015, but took first place in 2013 and 2014. In 2016, the award was renamed again to the Best FIFA Men's Player. Ronaldo won the award in 2016 and 2017.

In July 2008, Ronaldo became the Portuguese national team's permanent captain. In 2016, Ronaldo helped Portugal win its first-ever European Championship. Ronaldo said, "This is one of the happiest moments in my career." On January 6, 2013, he became one of Real Madrid's captains.

STAR POWER

In August 2016, he launched his CR7Selfie: Fans with a Cause app. Some of the money made from each download of the app is given to Save the Children.

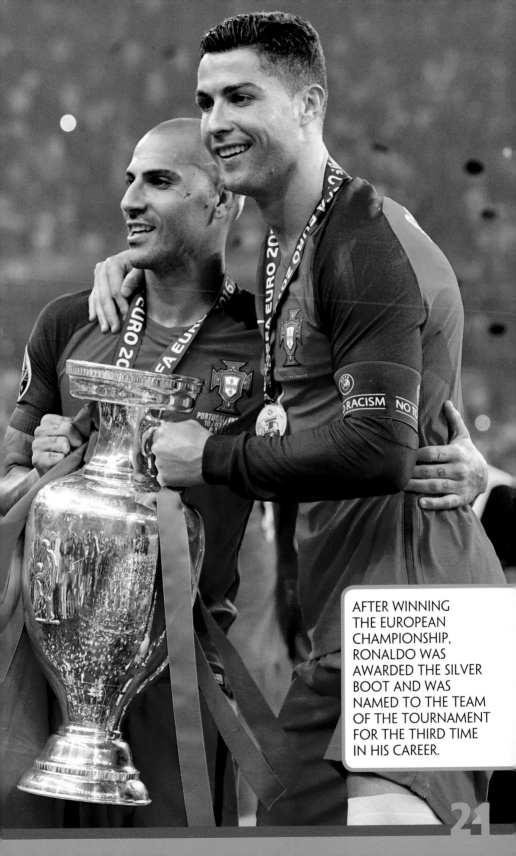

AFTER WINNING THE EUROPEAN CHAMPIONSHIP, RONALDO WAS AWARDED THE SILVER BOOT AND WAS NAMED TO THE TEAM OF THE TOURNAMENT FOR THE THIRD TIME IN HIS CAREER.

WHAT'S NEXT?

On March 18, 2018, when he was 32 years old, Ronaldo scored his 50th career **hat trick**. On April 8, 2018, he scored his 650th career goal. On April 11, 2018, he helped Real Madrid move on to the semifinal of the Champions League by scoring a winning goal against Juventus. This was his 10th goal against Juventus.

What's next for Cristiano Ronaldo? In 2018, he left Real Madrid to play for Juventus in Italy. For now, he doesn't have any plans to become a coach. Ronaldo just wants do what he loves. For Ronaldo, soccer is for life!

GLOSSARY

career: A period of time spent doing a job or activity.

challenge: Something that is hard to do.

compete: To try to win something, such as a prize or reward, that someone else is also trying to win.

elevate: To raise someone or something, such as a team, to a higher rank or level.

fee: An amount of money that must be paid.

foul: An action that is against the rules and for which a player is given a penalty.

generation: A group of people born and living at about the same time.

hat trick: The scoring of three goals in one game, such as soccer, by a single player.

humble: Low in rank or condition.

offense: A team or part of a team that attempts to score in a game.

professional: Having to do with a job someone does for a living, including being paid to participate in a sport.

rival: Someone or something that tries to defeat or be more successful than another person or thing.

INDEX

WEBSITES

Due to the changing nature of Internet links, PowerKids Press has
developed an online list of websites related to the subject of this book.
This site is updated regularly. Please use this link to access the list:
www.powerkidslinks.com/socstars/ronaldo